EMPATH

*The Empath's Survival Guide to Protect Yourself
from Narcissists & Negative Energy*

Sylvia Mitchell

© **Copyright 2020 All Rights Reserved.**

No part of this publication may be reproduced, distributed, or transmitted in any form or by any means, including photocopying, recording, or other electronic or mechanical methods, without the prior written permission of the publisher, except in the case of brief quotations embodied in reviews and certain other noncommercial uses permitted by copyright law.

Disclaimer: This book is designed to provide accurate and authoritative information in regard to the subject matter covered. By its sale, neither the publisher nor the author is engaged in rendering psychological or other professional services. If expert assistance or counseling is needed, the services of a competent professional should be sought.

Contents

Introduction	5
Chapter 1: What is an Empath?	7
Chapter 2: How to Embrace Your Gift	23
Chapter 3: Understanding Energy	27
Chapter 4: Empaths and Spiritual Hypersensitivity	35
Chapter 5: Empaths, Insomnia, Exhaustion and Adrenal Fatigue	49
Chapter 6: How to Protect Yourself from Energy Vampires	61
Chapter 7: Empaths and Work	67
Chapter 8: Normalizing and Maintaining Your Gift	77
Chapter 9: How to Support a Young Empath	83
Conclusion	93
Essential Oil Recipes for Anxiety	95

Introduction

Greetings readers! Congratulations on taking the first step on your journey to greatness as you begin to understand and use your gift for the greater good! If you are reading this, I can only assume that you are new and have just become conscious of your gift as an empath. You are probably both scared and excited; scared because you don't quite understand it and excited because you are about to step into a new realm of possibilities that you had no idea existed.

Empaths who are not in control of their gift find that it is a terrible source of stress, pain and anxiety. Feeling other people's emotions as though they are your own can seem as if you are on a constant emotional roller coaster. The purpose of this book is to bring you to a place of rest concerning the gift that you have been endowed with. You will learn exactly what your gift is and why you are so privileged to have it.

I want you to understand that you are carrying great power, and the reason why it affects you in such a profound way is due to the dynamism of it. There are many benefits and blessings associated with being an empath, and as you learn to walk in and embrace your gift, doors of opportunity will begin to open for you.

Take your time to fully understand and absorb each chapter before moving on to the next. Prepare your spirit for the keys that you are going to find in this book to unlock the abundance of potential that is within you.

In order to maximize the value you receive from this book, I highly encourage you to join our tight-knit community on Facebook. Here you will be able to connect and share with other like-minded Empaths to continue your growth.

Taking this journey alone is not recommended and this can be an excellent support network for you.

It would be great to connect with you there,

Chapter 1: What is an Empath?

An empath is a person with an open spirit; they unconsciously sense things in the unseen and the seen realm to the point where it can become a burden. They pick up on the energy that is surrounding them and have a natural ability to tune in to the feelings of others. They are influenced by other people's moods, thoughts, desires and wishes. Being an empath is not limited to high sensitivity and emotions; they intuitively know the intentions and motivations of others. An empath is not something that is learned; you are either born this way or you're not. As an empath, you are constantly in touch with the feelings and energy of others, which means that you are continuously bearing the weight of the emotions of those around you.

Many empaths are prone to the physical manifestations of the emotions they are burdened with, such as daily aches and pains and chronic tiredness. I am sure you have heard the saying, "You look like you're carrying the weight of the world on your shoulders!" This is exactly what empaths do! They carry the energy, emotions and karma of everyone they come in contact with.

Empaths are extremely humble; they shy away from compliments and would rather praise someone else than receive it. They express themselves with great passion and talk very candidly, which can sometimes cause offense. They are not the type of people who hide their feelings; they will open up to anyone who cares to listen.

On the flip side of this, they can also be the complete opposite; they can be very anti-social and will gladly block those out of their lives who they feel are hindering them in some way. They may not realize that they are doing this; to the empath who doesn't understand who they are, this is often their way of shutting out the feelings and energy from others that they constantly have to deal with.

Although empaths are sensitive to the emotions of others, they don't spend much time listening to their own hearts. This can lead them to care for the needs of others before their own. An empath is typically non-aggressive, non-violent and is quick to become the peacemaker between people. An empath feels extremely uncomfortable when they are in an environment of disharmony; they avoid confrontation or quickly make amends if a situation gets out of hand. If they lose control and say something that would cause offense, they resent themselves for it and will make a swift apology.

Empaths have a tendency to pick up the feelings of others and then project them back to the person without realizing what they are doing. When an empath is in the beginning stages of understanding their gift, it is advised that they talk things out in order to release the buildup of emotions. If not, they have a tendency to bottle things up and build skyscraper walls around themselves and refuse to let anyone in. The inability to express their feelings is often the result of a traumatic event, a childhood where emotions were not expressed in the home or having parents who told them that children are to be seen and not heard.

Emotional withdrawal can have a negative effect on our health; the longer we hold our emotions inside without release, the more power they have over us. When emotions build up, there will eventually be a release and that release is never a good thing. Humans are wired to express themselves when they feel a burden; it is how healing takes place. When you talk something out, there is an emotional relief that you are no longer carrying the weight alone. If this doesn't take place, there is a risk of mental and emotional instability as well as negative emotions manifesting in the form of an illness.

Empaths have sensitivity towards movies, TV, videos, and news broadcasts that depict scenes of violence or physical or emotional pain and trauma, whether it is an adult, child or animal. This can reduce them to tears and cause them to become physically ill. They are unable to justify the suffering that they feel and see and have no tolerance for others who don't share the same level of compassion as they do.

Empaths work in careers that enable them to help others, whether it's with animals, nature or people. They are passionate about their work and their dedication to others. You will often find empaths in volunteer positions dedicating their time to help others without pay or recognition.

Due to their ceaseless imagination, empaths are great storytellers; they are constantly learning and asking questions. They are also very gentle and romantic; they have a passion for family history and will keep old photos, jewelry or other items of value that have been passed down from generations. They are often the ones who sit and listen to stories told by grandparents and great grandparents and hold a wealth of knowledge about the history of their family.

To suit the variety of moods that they experience, they listen to a range of music genres. People are often curious about their taste in music, especially the extent of the diversity. One minute they are listening to classical music and the next hardcore rap! The lyrics to a song can have a powerful effect on an empath, especially if it relates to something they have recently experienced. It is advised that empaths listen to music without lyrics to avoid sending their emotions into a spin.

Empaths use their body language as a form of expression; they can articulate themselves just as easily through dance, body movements and acting as they can through words. Empaths are capable of exhibiting high amounts of energy when they dance; they get lost in the music and enter into a trance-like state as their spirits sync with the beat and the lyrics. They describe this feeling as becoming completely lost in the moment; they are no longer aware of the presence of others.

Empaths have very attractive spirits, and so people are naturally drawn to them without understanding why. They will find that complete strangers feel comfortable talking to them about the most intimate subjects and experiences. Another reason why empaths are so magnetic is that they are very good listeners; they are bubbly, outgoing, enthusiastic and people love to be in their presence. They are the life and soul of any party, and people like to have them around because they feed off their energy. Due to the extreme nature of their personality, the opposite is also true; their moods can switch in an instant and people will scatter like cockroaches to get away from them. If an empath doesn't understand their gift, the burden of carrying so many emotions can be overwhelming. They don't understand that they are feeling someone else's emotions; it is confusing to them. One moment they are fine and the next they are feeling a tsunami of depression, which causes them to act out.

It is not a good idea to abandon an empath in the heights of one of their mood swings. Whoever is around at this time should lend them a shoulder to cry on, become compassionate, and be a listening ear. This return of emphatic emotional care will often lead to an instant recovery. Empaths are often misunderstood, and it is a crucial part of their journey that not only do they understand themselves but others around them do too.

Empaths are often thinkers and problem solvers; they love to study a variety of different material. They believe that problems and solutions exist together and that there is always a solution at hand. They will often search until they find the answer to a problem, which can be a great benefit to others around them, whether at work or at home. The empath is often capable of tapping into the knowledge of the universe and receiving the guidance they need to solve the problem they have put their minds to.

Empaths are dreamers; they have vivid and detailed dreams. They believe that their dreams are linked to their physical reality and that they are being warned about something that is happening in their life or the life of someone they know. From a young age, they invest their time and effort into unlocking the mysteries of their dreams.

Empaths thrive off mental engagement; they have no desire for the mundane and find it difficult to hold their focus on things that don't stimulate them. When they find themselves getting bored, they will often resort to daydreaming and settle into a detached state of mind. Although their physical body is in the same location, their mind is in another dimension.

A teacher will only hold the attention of an empath student if they are as expressive and emotional as they are; if not they will quickly switch off. If empaths are not completely captivated by their audience, they lack interest. They make the best actors because of their innate ability to become so submerged by the feelings of others that when they play a role, they do so with all the emotions of the character that they are playing.

They are prone to experiencing synchronicities and déjà vu. What begins as a set of continuous coincidences leads to an understanding that seeing into the future is a part of who the empath is. As this acceptance becomes a reality, a feeling of euphoria sets in as they begin to connect with the power of their gift.

Many empaths have a deep connection to the paranormal; they will have a number of near-death and out of body experiences throughout their lives. Traveling in the spirit realm to another dimension is a normal occurrence in the life of an empath. They are free spirits and the mundane routine of life is not what they live for. When they get stuck in this cycle, all meaning of life is lost and they are forced to stop, re-examine their life and get back on the journey to self-discovery. Their paranormal experiences lead to isolation; to the average person this is not the norm and so the empath tends to suppress their abilities in fear of being labeled negatively. However, they are capable of overcoming this and it typically takes place when they are surrounded by other empaths.

There Are A Variety Of Empaths And Each Use A Different Psychic Emphatic Trait. They Are As Follows:

1. **Geomancy:** Geomancers have the ability to feel earth's energy; when they are on certain land and in certain places, they can feel the energy. When a natural disaster is about to take place, regardless of where it is happening, they get headaches.

2. **Telepathy:** They have the ability to read the thoughts of others.

3. **Psychometry:** They have the ability to receive energy from impressions, places, photographs or objects.

4. **Physical healing:** The ability to feel the physical symptoms of others in their

own body, which they can then use to promote healing.

5. **Animal communication:** The ability to feel, hear and communicate with animals.

6. **Emotional healing:** The ability to feel the emotions of others.

7. **Nature:** The ability to communicate with nature and plants.

8. **Mediumship:** The ability to feel the energy and the presence of spirits.

9. **Knowing or claircognizance:** The ability to know what has to be done in any given situation; this is often coupled with a feeling of calm and peace in the midst of a crisis.

10. **Precognition:** The ability to feel when something significant is about to take place. This is often an unexplainable feeling of doom or dread.

If You Are Unsure About Whether Or Not You Have The Gift Of An Empath, Here Are 25 Common Empath Traits:

1. They look for the victim, the underdog; those going through emotional trauma and suffering draws the attention of the empath.

2. The empath is highly creative with a vivid imagination; they are usually multitalented with the ability to sing, dance, draw, act or write. An untidy environment full of chaos and mess blocks the flow of energy for the empath; they are very minimalist and tidy.

3. They have a disdain for narcissism. Although empaths are very tolerant, compassionate and kind, they don't like to be around egotistical characters who live for themselves and have no consideration for the feelings and emotions of others.

4. They sense energy in food. Empaths are often vegetarian because they can feel the suffering that the animal experienced while being slaughtered.

5. They don't like buying second-hand goods, as they believe that anything previously owned by someone else

carries their energy. When the empath is financially stable, they prefer to buy a brand new house or a brand new car so that they are not stepping into someone else's energy.

6. They spend time daydreaming. An empath can get lost in their own imagination; they can happily stare into oblivion for hours. If an empath is not being stimulated, they get bored and distracted. Whether they are at home, work or school, they must be interested in what they are doing or they will drift.

7. They are knowledge seekers. Empaths are always learning something new; they find it frustrating when they have unanswered questions and they will go above and beyond the call of duty to find the answer. If they feel a nudge in their spirit that they have an answer, they will look for confirmation. The negative side of this is that they carry too much information, which can be draining. They have a deep desire to know more about the world as we know it.

8. They can't participate in what they don't enjoy. They feel as if they are not being truthful to themselves when they engage in activities that they don't like. Many empaths are labeled as lazy because they refuse to take part in anything that they

don't agree with, and that happens to be the majority of things.

9. The need for isolation. They must get time alone, which is even true of empath children.

10. They have a love of animals and nature. Empaths enjoy life outdoors and being at one with nature. They typically have pets inside the home. They believe that plants and animals have feelings and emotions.

11. They are very much in touch with the supernatural realm and things like seeing ghosts and spirits are normal to them. They also seem to have access to information that scientists will spend years trying to attain. For example, empaths knew that the world was round when everyone else believed that it was flat.

12. They are always tired; because they are so exposed to other people's energy, they constantly feel drained and tired. This tiredness is so extreme that even sleep can't relieve them. Empaths are often diagnosed with Myalgic Encephalomyelitis (ME). They suffer from back problems and digestive disorders. The center of the abdomen is where the solar plexus chakra is located.

Empaths feel the emotions of others in this area, which weakens it and can lead to irritable bowel syndrome, stomach ulcers and lower back problems. The empath who doesn't understand their gift will typically suffer from such physical problems. They catch illnesses quickly; an empath develops the physical symptoms of those around them. They often catch the flu, eye infections, and aches and pains in the body and joints. When they are close to someone, they often experience sympathy pains.

13. The empath is a sounding board. Everyone goes to the empath to unload their problems, which often end up as their own. They feel and take on others' emotions. They can feel emotions of those close by, far away or both. The more experienced empath knows when someone is thinking badly about them.

14. They can detect lies. When someone is not telling the truth, the empath is aware, and when someone is thinking or feeling one way but saying something else, they know. They don't need to listen to the tone of someone's voice or analyze their facial expressions to know that they are lying; they have the ability to know instantly whether or not they are lying.

15. They find it difficult to watch any type of violence. Neither can they read about it in newspapers and magazines; as a result of this, empaths find it difficult to watch TV or read newspapers and magazines.

16. They are often overwhelmed in public places. Being in places like supermarkets, stadiums and shopping malls where there are a lot of people is difficult for the empath because of the amount of energy that is being released from the crowds. Their environment is arranged and managed to work around their sensitivities. Their schedule and commitments are arranged to avoid chaotic, unpleasant situations that are overly stimulating.

17. They have access to advanced knowledge. Empaths are tuned into knowledge; they know things without being told. This is not a gut feeling or intuition, their knowledge comes from a greater source of power. The more they are tuned into their gift, the stronger this gift becomes.

18. They are capable of influencing the moods of others. They are very charismatic and people are attracted to their energy. When they spend too much

time around people, they start to speak and act like them.

19. They like to be around water; they enjoy the energy from oceans, rivers, and seas.

20. They have always been told that they are too emotional and sensitive. Their ability to pick up on feelings and cues is not normal to everyone else, but it is to them.

21. They have a low tolerance for pain; they find it difficult to get injections and feel ill when they have to deal with even the smallest of injuries. Doctors may even tell them that they complain too much.

22. They are very observant and extremely good at reading facial expressions and body language.

23. They are drawn to healing professions; empaths are often nurses, doctors or veterinarians. Empaths are drawn to become counselors, social workers, psychologists, animal communicators, teachers and caretakers.

24. Empaths are drawn to alternative and spiritual arts such as organic nutrition, hypnotherapy, psychotherapy, holistic, energy and Reiki practices and psychic reading. They have an interest in the metaphysical such as prayer, meditation, yoga and positive affirmations.

25. They are non-conformists and choose to live outside of the constraints of society's norm of a job—a family and 2.4 children. They enjoy traveling, adventure and freedom. Empaths are free spirits; they don't like to remain stagnant. They don't like rules, routine or control. An empath likes to have the freedom to do what they want to do when they want to do it. If they are unable to do so, they feel restricted and imprisoned.

Chapter 2: How to Embrace Your Gift

As you have read, being an empath is physically and emotionally exhausting, which can cause you to feel as if you don't have a gift but a burden. Feeling this burden is the first step towards embracing your gift. You will now need to learn how to look after yourself so that you can embrace your gift without feeling exhausted. This is an extremely important process and you should invest time and effort into mastering the best techniques for effective coping mechanisms. Once you learn how to cope and function as an empath, you can use your gift to better yourself and your environment.

Due to the constant feelings of overwhelming emotions and stress, you must go to great lengths to eliminate the negative energy that you can attract. The techniques that you learn should become a part of your daily routine and will open your eyes to the true value of the gift that you have been blessed with.

Even though being an empath is not a disease or a curse, it is controversial and can cause you to feel so uncomfortable that you will try to suppress it. In alcoholics or narcotics anonymous their slogan is the first step to cure is to admit that you have a problem. The same applies to you as an empath; the first step towards embracing your gift is admitting that you are indeed an empath and that you are proud of it. Although this is a small step, it will make a great difference, as you will eliminate a lot of the stress associated with hiding your gift.

In order for you to feel relieved from the struggles of being an empath, it is essential that you get enough rest. The most effective method of doing so is to set a regular sleep-wake cycle and do what you can to ensure that you have a restful sleep throughout the night (see chapter 5). You should also take regular breaks throughout the day for relaxation and deep breathing exercises to rid yourself of some of the stress that has built up throughout the day. Such exercises will provide you with immediate relief (see chapter 7).

Take care that you do not place yourself in environments that are overly stimulating on a regular basis. It can be difficult to avoid them completely; however, you should endeavor to avoid them as much as you can. If you know that you are going to be in an overly stimulating environment, make sure that you prepare yourself emotionally and mentally beforehand. This will enable you to quickly rid yourself of any of the stress that you feel as a result of the energy that you are surrounded by.

Social media and the internet in general are extremely stimulating environments. It is advised that you often take a break from the energy that is emitted through the internet. You don't have to be in the physical presence of someone to absorb their energy.

It is also advised that you have a regular routine in place for stress relief. What you do depends on what you find relaxing. You might enjoy reading motivational books, getting a massage, going to a spa, using aromatherapy or taking a warm bath.

HERE ARE SOME HELPFUL TIPS TO ASSIST YOU IN FULLY EMBRACING YOUR GIFT:

APPRECIATE AND HONOR YOUR STATE OF CONSCIOUSNESS

Empaths often feel pressure because they are different. Being different brings many challenges because the world expects you to conform to its norms and values. When you are misunderstood by others, it is easy to take their disapproval personal and carry it as a burden. It is normal to be emphatic and a gift to be in tune with yourself physically and spiritually. I would go as far as saying that it is essential that you have this gift to survive because it puts you on high alert when danger is surrounding you or your family.

IDENTIFY THE DIFFERENCE BETWEEN THOUGHT CONSCIOUSNESS AND EMPHATIC CONSCIOUSNESS

You can observe the difference between day and night because you can see it. It is difficult to identify emphatic awareness because you can't see it. It is something that is felt and experienced on the inside. Once you can identify this difference, you will begin to see your gift as a blessing instead of a curse. You attain self-knowledge when you know when the mind and its thoughts are dominating. Feelings and thoughts are different, and when you recognize these differences, you will feel liberated. This knowledge will give you the power to defend yourself against energetic tides instead of being pulled into them.

TRUST IN YOUR INTUITION

The majority of empaths awakening to their gifts ignore their gut instincts. Don't do this; your intuition is always correct. This does not mean that you should fully understand or embrace the feeling. You may not have complete knowledge of the situation, but the feeling is real and you should embrace the deeper communication that is happening within.

Chapter 3: Understanding Energy

Once an empath starts to embrace their gift and understand that they don't have to carry other people's energy around with them, a natural curiosity about energy sets in. Through your symptoms and experiences, you are aware of how powerfully energy can affect you in a negative way. If this is the case, it is also possible that energy can have a positive effect on you. Once you have learned how to deal with the stress of carrying energy, it then frees you to learn how you can use energy positively. Learning how energy works is an exciting adventure, and it can take you to places in life that you didn't think existed. As you have read, many empaths become healers; these are the people who have learned how to embrace their gift because they understand how their energy can have a positive effect on others.

The first step in learning about energy is to understand how to ground yourself from different energy. This will help you to avoid becoming overwhelmed by the energy that you can feel. One of the most popular grounding techniques is through visualization. This is where you consciously imagine yourself being grounded; here are some steps to get you started:

Sit comfortably in a chair and position both of your feet firmly on the ground with your palms facing upwards. Don't force yourself into a certain position; simply allow your body to relax into the chair. Imagine that a piercing white light is radiating from the sun and through your crown chakra and leaving the bottom of your spine and then into the earth's center. Imagine that as your body is being filled with the white light, negative black energy is being released through your palms. When your entire body has been filled with the white light you will naturally relax knowing that you are now filled with positive and peaceful energy.

You should practice visualization on a regular basis as a strategy to keep you grounded to the earth underneath you, to release the negative energy that has attached itself to you and to enhance your empath gift.

Working confidently with energy will cause you to stop feeling as if you are out of control. It will enable you to protect yourself and heal yourself and the people who are placed in your path. Ultimately, it will give you the ability to control the energy that is directly affecting you.

There are many things that you can excel in when you learn to effectively handle energy, which is one of the reasons it is so attractive to many. It is your divine right to learn how to navigate this powerful terrain of energy so that you can use it in a way that benefits you and others.

Mediumistic Abilities

A medium uses their intuitive or psychic abilities to see into the past, present and future of an individual's life by tuning into the spirit energy surrounding that person. Mediums are reliant upon the presence of a spiritual energy outside of themselves to gain accurate information about the person they are reading. In the work of mediumship, a connection is made with the dead to deliver messages to those who are alive. Information is received directly from the dead, angels and spirit guides. There are four main types of mediumship:

Clairsentience

You strongly sense the emotions and feelings of people, spirits, animals and places. You feel these emotions both in your heart and in your body; you also feel the presence of spirits. If you have clairsentient abilities:

- You are very sensitive to your surroundings; you easily sense the vibe of a person or place.

- You have unexplainable physical or emotional reactions when you go to places where there are large crowds.

- Your emotions change suddenly when you are around people or when you arrive at a person's home.

- You know what people are feeling without them telling you; you can empathize with people easily.

- You can feel the presence of spirits.

- When people are in pain, you can feel it in your own body.

- You use the words "I feel" when you are having conversations with others.

- You can taste and smell things from the spirit world.

Claircognizance

Information comes to you spontaneously; you don't doubt it and believe in your soul that it is 100 percent accurate. This information will either come in the form of figures and facts, or you just know the truth of a situation, a girlfriend/boyfriend or a career path. If you have claircognizant abilities:

- You receive the answers to things and don't understand how or where it came from.

- You have very inspirational, creative and beneficial ideas.

- Your mind is never still; you are always coming up with a new idea, especially when you are working on a project.

- You automatically know when someone is telling the truth or not.

- You tend to use the words "I know" when having conversations with others.

Clairvoyance

You see things as images in your mind or as a precognition in dreams before they manifest. If you have clairvoyant abilities:

- You constantly have very vivid dreams.

- Are very imaginative and spend a lot of time daydreaming.

- Always speak in metaphors.

- You can see shapes, colors, pictures or objects when you close your eyes to sleep or during meditation.

- You see flashes of light, sparkly lights, or movements through the corners of your eyes.

- You often use the words "I see" when you are talking to others.

CLAIRAUDIENCE

You hear messages either inside your mind or audibly. For the majority of people, these messages come in the form of telepathic communication, meaning that the spirits will have a conversation with you through your thoughts. You can have a conversation with the spirits and they will reply. If you have clairaudient traits:

- You listen more than you talk.

- You speak to plants and animals because you believe that they can communicate with you.

- You often feel as if you are the recipient of telepathic information.

- When you provide really helpful advice, you forget what you said straight away and wonder where you got such wise information.

- You often hear buzzing or ringing in your ears. You experience the same sensation in your ears just before they pop on an airplane.

- You use the words "I hear" when speaking to people.

Due to the intuitive nature of empaths, they are often drawn to mediumistic abilities. This is not a natural trait of an empath, but that doesn't mean that you can't have the gift; it is in fact easier for an empath to develop this gift because of their sensitivity to the spirit world. If you feel that you are being drawn to this area and you decide that you want to develop this skill, it is not something that you should take lightly and is crucial that you find a good teacher. As you have now learned, empaths absorb all types of energy, whether positive or negative, and if you get in contact with the wrong spirit, it will torment you.

Psychic Abilities

Empaths are capable of sensing things before they manifest; the psychic ability is strongly connected to your ability to "just know." You will often have visions or premonitions about things prior to them happening. You can't learn to have visions or premonitions, but you can train yourself to have them whenever you need to. This provides you with the wonderful and powerful ability to be able to predict future events. You may not have experienced any premonitions or visions yet, but this doesn't mean that you can't operate in that gift; it may be that you haven't tapped into it yet. As you learn how to control this gift, you will find it easy and exciting to predict the future.

Energy Projection

One of the things that you may not be aware of as an empath is that you can send energy to people. When you do so you are giving that individual the particular sensation or vibe that you want them to experience. This is a skill that is used for remote healing, where empaths are capable of healing people when they are not even in their presence. Others use this as a way of praying for people and sending good energy and thoughts in the direction of another person to help them to get through a difficult time when they are unable to be there personally. Sending energy is not limited to empaths; everyone can do this if they put their mind to it. However, when empaths send energy the recipient is more likely to feel it because they have a powerful connection to the energy source.

Healing

Empaths understand the connection that energy and people have, this is referred to as an energy body, and it can become inflicted with illness or pain. When you are trained in energy healing, you learn how you can work with your own or another person's energy body to induce healing to create a healthy energy body.

Chapter 4: Empaths and Spiritual Hypersensitivity

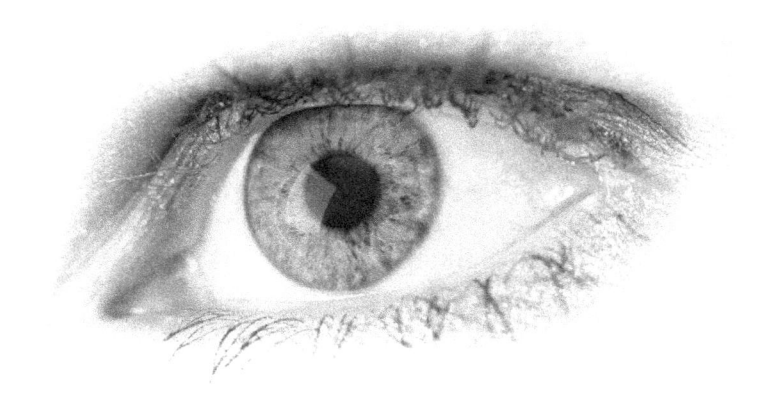

Empaths often suffer from spiritual based hypersensitivity; the symptoms include:

- Your environment causes you to feel overwhelmed
- Sounds are too loud, even if made at a normal range
- You constantly feel the feelings of others

This type of energetic overwhelm is nothing new; the spiritual community has been dealing with it for many years. As more and more empaths choose to ignore their gift, they are becoming less connected with the universe, which has led to an increase in spiritual based hypersensitivity. Oversensitivity to people's energy and noise is a common reaction to energy acceleration, as you ascend to higher heights in your spiritual development, you should expect to experience this. When you begin to accelerate in the spiritual realm, you may feel like a radio signal picking up a million signals at once. When there is a shift in spiritual vibration, your sense of intuition and your emphatic channels are open causing a heightened awareness of the thoughts and feelings of those around you. Spiritual hypersensitivity can manifest physically causing third eye dizziness, hypersensitivity to energy, odors, light and noise.

Metaphysics believes that the body is a vehicle for the spirit, the body is not who we are; our person is carried in our spirit. Wayne Dyer states that we are spiritual beings living in a physical world. Everything that happens in the physical first happens in the realm of the spirit; therefore, if there is an imbalance in your spirit it will manifest through your physical body. Metaphysical wellness counselors always address the spiritual aspects of healing before focusing on the physical, and it is spiritual alignment that cures the physical ailments.

HOW TO COPE WITH SPIRITUAL HYPERSENSITIVITY

When the body is overwhelmed physically, emotionally or mentally, the fight or flight syndrome is activated and breathing becomes shallow. When you begin to experience a change in your breathing pattern, you should immediately start practicing conscious breathing. This is where you focus your attention on your breath, which will slow down your nervous system and allow you to relax. Breathe slowly, deeply and in a rhythm at the same time as focusing your mind on being able to relax in the situation that you are in. You should always take a temporary retreat from any stressful situation such as family or work-related conflicts. Excusing yourself to the bathroom is a good way to do this. This will allow you to get away from the negative energy, practice your breathing techniques and renew yourself.

THERE ARE ALSO SEVERAL SPIRITUAL HEALING TOOLS THAT YOU CAN USE:

PRAYER

Depending on what you believe in, prayer can always bring comfort in an overwhelming situation. One of the most talked about and effective prayers is the H'oponopono prayer. Here is the story behind it.

The Hawaii State Hospital for the criminally insane was a clinic for those who had committed the most heinous of crimes. Criminals who had committed murder, kidnap, rape or other crimes of such magnitude were either sent there because of their mental condition or to determine whether they were sane enough to stand trial. According to one of the nurses who worked there, it was a place with no hope; the atmosphere was so congested with evil and negativity that not even paint wanted to reside in the building and would not stick to the walls. Everything was rotting, decaying, repulsive and terrifying. Not a day would go by without someone being physically attacked.

The doctors and nurses were bound by fear; when an inmate was walking in their direction, even though they were shackled hand and foot, they would walk as close to the walls as possible to keep away from them. However, not even shackles could stop the attacks, and so the inmates were never taken outside unless it was an absolute emergency. Staff were absent the majority of the time and would often take sick leave to escape the depressing and dangerous environment that they were working in.

Every few months, a new doctor was hired because they were unable to handle the inmates, but one day Dr. Stanley Hew Len entered the clinic. The nurses were not at all enthusiastic; they were convinced he would be like the rest and bombard them with his supposed superior strategy that would get the place in order and then leave within a few months when he realized the reality of the situation he had got himself into. They soon discovered that everything about this doctor was different; he wasn't doing anything significant, but his demeanor didn't fit the environment. Where everyone else was depressed and angry, he was always naturally relaxed, cheerful and smiling. Every so often, he would ask for the files of the inmates; he rarely saw them personally, but he would sit in his office and look over their files. To the members of staff who were interested in the way he chose to operate, he would tell them about something he referred to as H'oponopono. As the months went by, things started to change in the hospital, the walls were painted and the paint actually remained on the walls, which gave the place some life. The gardens were being pruned, the tennis courts were repaired and prisoners who ordinarily were never allowed to go outside began to play tennis with the staff. They began to allow some of the prisoners to move around without their shackles and the inmates started to take fewer psychotropic medications.

The shift in the atmosphere was astounding; the staff began to come to work, and where there was once a shortage of applicants, there was now a high demand to work at the clinic and they slowly began to release the prisoners. Dr. Hew Len was employed by the clinic for almost four years; by the time he left, there were only a few inmates remaining who were eventually housed in another location because the clinic had to close, as the prisoners no longer required their services.

It appeared that Dr. Hew Len didn't apply any specific technique or give the prisoners any medication. All he seemed to do was look at their files, but what he did do was heal himself with a traditional Hawaiian spiritual remedy referred to as

H'oponopono. In Dr. Len's own words, "I was healing the part of me that created them."

While he sat in his office looking at each individual patient file, he would feel pain and empathy towards them. Dr. Len would then use what he was feeling to heal himself, taking on full responsibility for what each patient appeared to be going through. The prisoners were healed because their doctor took on their pain and healed them through himself.

H'oponopono is based on the belief that we create our own environment; there are no external forces responsible for what is taking place within our surroundings. If your boss is evil, you are responsible. If your children are not doing well in school, you are responsible. World wars and poverty are your responsibility. The bottom line is that the world belongs to you and it is your responsibility to take care of it. Taking responsibility doesn't mean that the problems are your fault, it simply means that you need to heal yourself in order to heal the situation that you find distressing.

Some may agree with this theology, and to others it may appear completely nonsensical; but if you really choose to analyze it, you will find that your perception of the world is your reality. If you think the world is depressive and pointless because you choose to focus on all of the negative that is surrounding you, that's how you perceive the world. You could change it if you would focus on changing yourself. Two people can live in the same environment but perceive it completely differently simply because of their perception.

So how can you heal yourself with H'oponopono? There are four steps to the concept:

- **Repent:** Say you are sorry for the part that you have played in the things you perceive as evil or problematic that are surrounding you. As an empath you can say that you are sorry for the pain that the people you have met recently are experiencing. Whatever you feel responsible for, say you are sorry for it; feel the remorse and mean it.

- **Ask for Forgiveness:** You are probably wondering, "Well, who am I asking?" We all have our different belief systems. The majority of us and especially empaths believe in some kind of higher power and so that is who you ask to forgive you.

- **Gratitude:** Say thank you; there is so much power in gratitude. If you take your focus off the negative, you will find that you have so many things to be thankful for. Say thank you that you woke up this morning. Say thank you that you have eyes to see, a nose to smell, legs to walk on, that your internal organs are all in working order. Find something to say thank you for and say it continuously.

- **Love:** Love is the most powerful force in the universe; saying the words, "I love you" over and over again will bring love into your life. You can say I love you to your cat, your house, your car, the sky, the trees! Whatever you feel love towards, say it.

WATER

Water has extraordinary balancing and healing properties during times of hypersensitivity. When consumed with consciousness, it provides inner alignment. You can balance the surrounding energy by putting a drop of water on your third eye area. When you apply water that you have energized, it leads to even more powerful results. You can energize water by praying over it, or putting a word on the bottle with the intention of infusing the words frequency into the bottle. Words such as healing, calmness, and peace work well.

Taking a hot shower works well for aura cleansing and for the restoration of energetic balance. Take a shower and imagine the water washing away negative feelings, impressions and thoughts from others and envision all of the negative energy being sucked down the drain.

Mindfulness

This technique can pull calming energy into the body. Focus on your breath at the same time as looking at something beautiful like a rose, the sun or the sky. You can even focus on the palm of your hands as if this is the first time you have seen them. You can redirect the attention you are paying to your feelings by focusing on something visual.

Essential Oils

Essential oils have a calming effect and can greatly improve the anxiety associated with spiritual hypersensitivity. The American College of Healthcare Sciences conducted a study in 2014, in which 58 hospice patients were given a daily hand massage for one week using a blend of essential oils. The oil blend was made up of lavender, frankincense and bergamot. All patients reported less depression and pain as a result of the essential oil massages. The study concluded that essential oil blend aromatherapy massages were more effective for depression and pain management than massage alone.

The following are some of the best oils for treating anxiety:

LAVENDER

Lavender oil has a relaxing and calming effect; it restores the nervous system, provides inner peace, better sleep, causes a reduction in restlessness, panic attacks, irritability and general nervous tension. There have been several clinical studies proving that inhaling lavender causes an immediate reduction in anxiety and stress. One study discovered that taking lavender oil capsules orally led to an increase in heart rate variation in comparison to the placebo while watching a film that caused anxiety. The study concluded that lavender had an anxiolytic effect, which means that it has the ability to inhibit anxiety.

Other studies have concluded that lavender has the ability to reduce anxiety in patients having coronary artery bypass surgery and in patients who are afraid of the dentist.

ROSE

Rose alleviates depression, anxiety, grieving, shock and panic attacks. The Iranian Red Crescent Medical Journal published a study in which a group of women experiencing their first pregnancy inhaled rose oil for 10 minutes at the same time as having a footbath. A second group of women experiencing pregnancy for the first time was also given the footbath but without the rose oil inhalation. The results discovered that a footbath combined with aromatherapy caused a reduction in anxiety in nulliparous (a woman that has not had any children yet) women in the active phase.

VETIVER

Vetiver oil contains reassuring, grounding and tranquil energy. It is often used for patients experiencing trauma and helps with stabilization and self-awareness. It also has a calming effect. Vetiver oil is a nervous system tonic; it reduces hypersensitivity, jitteriness, shock and panic attacks. The Natural Product Research published a study that examined rats with anxiety disorders and found that vetiver oil caused a reduction in anxiety.

YLANG YLANG

Ylang ylang has a calming and uplifting effect; it improves depression and anxiety due to its ability to induce optimism, cheerfulness, and courage. Ylang ylang also soothes fear, nervous palpitations and heart agitation. It is also a sedative that helps with insomnia.

A 2006 study conducted in Korea by Geochang Provincial College found that using a combination of ylang ylang, lavender and bergamot oil for four weeks once a day caused a reduction in blood pressure, hypertension, serum cortisol levels, and psychological stress responses.

BERGAMOT OIL

Bergamot is one of the ingredients in Earl Grey tea and has a distinctive floral aroma and taste. Bergamot oil provides soothing energy that reduces depression, agitation, induces relaxation and helps with insomnia. A study conducted in 2011 discovered that the application of bergamot oil reduced anxiety, depression, blood pressure and pulse rate.

CHAMOMILE

Chamomile oil is known for its calming effect and its ability to produce inner peace, reduce worry, anxiety, over-thinking and irritability. The University of Pennsylvania School of Medicine conducted an explorative study and found that it contains medicinal anti-depressant properties. The National Center for Complementary and Integrative Health also found that chamomile capsules have the ability to reduce anxiety related symptoms.

FRANKINCENSE

Frankincense oil is great for treating anxiety and depression due to its tranquil energy and calming effects. It also helps you focus, quiet the mind and deepen meditation. A Keimyung University study in Korea found that a combination of lavender, frankincense and bergamot reduced pain and depression in hospice patients suffering from terminal cancer.

How to Use Essential Oils for Hypersensitivity

Essential oils are either ingested, applied topically or used in aromatherapy. Here are some suggestions for their usage:

Aromatherapy

Aromatherapy is a very popular remedy for anxiety because of the human ability to process information through smell; it can trigger a very powerful emotional response. There is a region in the brain called the limbic system that controls memory recall and emotional processing. Inhaling the scent of essential oils stimulates a mental response in the brain's limbic system, which regulates stress and calming responses such as the production of hormones, blood pressure and breathing patterns. You can use the oils in the bath, a hot water vapor, direct inhalation, a humidifier or vaporizer, cologne, perfume, a vent or aromatherapy diffusers.

Oral Application

You can consume the majority of essential oils orally. However, it is essential that the oils you use are safe and pure. The majority of commercialized oils have been blended with synthetics or diluted with other substances making them unsafe for ingesting. The most effective method for consuming essential oils is to combine a drop of oil with a teaspoon of honey or drop the oil into a glass of water. You can also add a couple of drops to the food you are cooking. You can place a couple of drops under your tongue. This is particularly beneficial because the blood capillaries are located under the tongue near the surface of the tissue, which allows the oil to quickly absorb into the bloodstream and travel to the area of the body where it is required. You can also take essential oils in capsule form.

TOPICAL APPLICATION

Topical application is the process of placing essential oils on the skin, nails, teeth, hair or mucous membranes of the body. The oils are quickly absorbed by the skin. Due to the strength of the oils, it is essential that you dilute or blend them with a carrier oil such as coconut, avocado, jojoba, or sweet almond oil. You can apply the blended mixture directly to the affected area, around the rims of the ears, the soles of the feet, in the bath, through a warm compress, or through a massage.

To learn more about how to optimize essential oils in your life, refer to the end of the book where I've included four high quality essential oil recipes to relieve anxiety.

Chapter 5: Empaths, Insomnia, Exhaustion and Adrenal Fatigue

Due to the emotional responsibilities that empaths carry, they often experience a sudden drop in energy, which leads to chronic fatigue. When an empath does not remain grounded, balanced and consciously aware, they can unconsciously give their energy to others. When an empath spends too much time in the company of negative or depressed people, they take on their energy, and this can lead to emotional exhaustion. This is one of the main reasons they must spend time alone as a way of recharging their internal batteries.

The mind, soul and body are connected; whatever we think and feel has an effect on our physical body. An empath must have regular periods of isolation throughout the day in order to process feelings and emotions. This prevents emotional exhaustion, which then enables them to constantly let go of crushing negative energy. If an empath does not do this, they find it difficult to sleep at night because their minds are unable to process and make sense of the information that took place during the day. This hyperactive mindset causes empaths to become extremely tired. If it is not possible for the empath to find solitude during the day, it is essential that they meditate before they go to bed so that they can release any emotions they have come into contact with throughout the day.

EFFECTS OF THE ADRENAL GLANDS

Negative feelings can lead to the empath experiencing fear, resentment, anxiety, paranoia and panic, and they become genuinely convinced that something bad is going to happen to them. These thoughts send signals to the adrenal glands, which produce hormones that release excess amounts of energy. Not enough sleep, too much work, bad diet, bad relationships, and family problems all have a negative effect on the adrenal glands. The adrenal glands are shaped like the kidneys but are approximately the size of a walnut. They are located just above the kidneys in the lower back area. The adrenal glands are of great benefit when we are under stress because they assist in keeping us focused and alert and they increase our levels of stamina, which enables us to handle pressure.

However, when the adrenal glands are over stimulated, they continue to produce energy, which is what prevents us from being able to sleep. The mind and body stay on high alert, which causes excess stress on the adrenal glands and will eventually cause them to malfunction. A lack of energy leads to a craving for foods that are high in sugar and refined salt, which quickly turn into energy giving the body an instant but short-lived energy boost.

The body naturally craves sugar and salt. However, we tend to feed it with refined sugar and salt, which is found in the majority of junk and processed foods. In excess amounts, these foods can cause a range of different health problems. Unrefined sugar and salt is nutritious in healthy doses and can replenish and nourish the adrenal glands.

When the adrenal glands are not functioning properly, you will feel tired, groggy, anxious, irritable, overwhelmed and dizzy. You may also experience heart palpitations, high or low blood pressure, salt and sugar cravings as well as find it difficult to handle times of stress. If our bodies are in harmony, a good diet, sleeping well and positive thoughts, the adrenal glands are not overwhelmed easily. Cortisol is a hormone produced by the adrenal glands; during sleep our cortisol levels rise and peak a few hours before daybreak. This is how the body naturally prepares itself for the day and it is referred to as the circadian rhythm. It increases our energy levels so we are capable of functioning throughout the day. When the adrenal glands are overworked, we wake up feeling exhausted even if we have had the normal eight hours of sleep. We feel tired throughout the day, which then causes our cortisol levels to peak in the evening, making it hard for us to sleep properly.

Keeping the adrenal glands in a healthy state

It takes a long time to destroy the adrenal glands, and it will take the same amount of time to repair it. However, there are some changes that we can make in our lives that will help immediately. It is essential that we spend time listening to our body so that we are aware of how it feels at any given moment. This allows us to keep track of our energy levels throughout the day. You may find that your energy levels fluctuate throughout the day and that there are certain times of the day when your energy levels drop the most. It is imperative that you understand why so much stress is being placed on the adrenal glands. When the root cause of the problem is identified, we can ensure that we don't remain in that heightened state that causes further strain on the adrenal glands.

Meditation is a powerful tool for emptying the mind and spirit of negative emotions. It also helps us focus on the body so that we are aware of any physical sensations that are taking place. When we feel isolated, lonely and separated, cortisol levels can increase; you can combat this by spending time with friends and family. However, if you are the type of person who likes spending time alone and you enjoy your own company, periods of isolation is not a problem.

Diet and exercise can have a negative effect on the adrenal gland. It is not a good idea to push too hard during a workout; your body will tell you when it has had enough, and it is essential that you stop at this point or you will cause the adrenal glands to produce excess stress-related hormones.

Eating junk food, skipping meals and hardcore workouts all cause the adrenal glands to overwork. To keep the adrenal glands in a healthy state, we should eat an organic, nutritional and well-balanced diet with the daily protein requirements, with vitamins A, B, and C. You should refrain from excess alcohol and preferably eliminate refined salt, sugar and caffeine intake. A healthy state of mind where you feel peaceful and content with life and getting enough sleep at night all contribute to healthy adrenal glands.

Why Cut Out Refined Salt?

Research conducted by the director of the University of Washington in Seattle found that low sodium levels cause a reduction in blood volume. The body compensates by activating the sympathetic nervous system, which releases adrenaline triggering the fight or flight response, which makes sleep difficult.

Why Cut Out Refined Sugar?

When the adrenals have been overworked, it can cause interrupted sleep patterns often from vivid dreams, all of which can cause heightened anxiety. Stress and anxiety contribute to sleepless nights due to excess adrenaline; this typically takes place between 2:00 and 4:00 a.m. The surge of hormones makes it difficult for us to remain calm and wakes the body up in an agitated state.

Here is a natural remedy that will assist in eliminating this problem:

Honey and Salt

Combine five teaspoons of raw organic honey with 1 teaspoon of Himalayan rock salt. Twenty minutes before going to bed, place a small amount under the tongue and let it dissolve. The combination of salt and honey naturally de-stresses the body through hormone regulation. This results in a harmonious, peaceful and restful state, which prepares the body for a deep sleep. Honey and salt also sustains the body, preventing you from waking up feeling hungry during the night.

Those who consume honey and salt before going to bed have reported that they no longer experience sleep deprivation; they sleep throughout the night and wake up energized and refreshed and no longer experience dips in energy throughout the day. Bedtime anxiety has now been replaced with peace and tranquility knowing that they will be asleep within minutes and remain in a sound smooth sleep until the morning.

THE BENEFITS OF RAW ORGANIC HONEY:

Honey aids in releasing liver glycogen in the brain. A lack of liver glycogen causes the adrenal glands to produce the stress hormones cortisol and adrenaline. One of the ingredients in honey is tryptophan, which is responsible for producing serotonin, a hormone that induces relaxation. When there is no light, serotonin is converted to melatonin, which causes restorative sleep.

Melatonin regulates the sleep-wake cycle as it works in harmony with the morning and night. When our melatonin levels are stable, we fall asleep easily and naturally when it gets dark and when light starts to enter the room, our body automatically wakes up.

We have been taught to believe that salt is bad for the health; this statement is not entirely true. A healthy balance of the right salt stabilizes the metabolism. It is essential that we have a healthy metabolism, as it is required to ensure that the food we eat is absorbed and turned into energy. Salt contains anti-excitatory and anti-stress properties, which reduces our stress levels and helps us to remain calm.

We often have a craving for salt not realizing that it eliminates anxiety and creates an overall sense of well-being. Unfortunately, when this need arises the majority of us will consume processed foods containing refined table salts, which have no health benefits. When we start consuming unrefined salts such as Celtic, Himalayan or Real salt, we immediately notice that our stress levels go down, our energy levels are increased and we have a clear mental and emotional state.

Another myth is that eating after 7 p.m. causes weight gain; there is no scientific evidence to prove this. However, there is evidence to suggest that an evening snack helps us to stay asleep because when we get hungry, the adrenal stress hormone is activated by the brain, which then puts us on the fight or flight alert.

BENEFITS OF A HIMALAYAN SALT LAMP

A Himalayan salt lamp is a huge piece of pure Himalayan Salt with a small bulb on the inside. It provides a subtle warm glow that improves the quality of the air. Mobile phones and laptops release an overload of positive ions into the air. A Himalayan salt lamp will make you feel happier and create a sense of calmness and freshness to the air as the ions are balanced out. An ion is a molecule or atom in which the sum of the electrons is not equal to the sum of the protons; this gives the atom a net negative or positive electrical charge.

Cations are also referred to as positive charged ions, and anions are also referred to as negative charged ions. The combination of negative and positive charged ions enables them to bond and move around in the atmosphere.

Negative ions are typically created by sunlight, lightning storms, ocean waves and waterfalls. According to Pierce J. Howard, the author of "The Owner's Manual for the Brain," there are several benefits associated with negative ions. They cause more oxygen to flow to the brain, which results in less drowsiness, more mental energy and alertness. They protect against germs in the atmosphere that cause sneezing, throat irritation and coughing. One in three people are sensitive to the effectiveness of negative ions and can make people feel refreshed instantly.

The best way to get negative ion exposure is to spend time outdoors, especially around water. Himalayan salt lamps produce small amounts of negative ions. Positive ions are generated by electronic devices such as microwaves, TVs, computers, and vacuum cleaners. They can cause and intensify health problems such as sleep deprivation, allergies and stress. Negative and positive ions bond together, which causes the negative ions to neutralize the positive ions. This process helps to cleanse the air. Salt lamps also provide a soft glow, which many people find relaxing.

Salt is hygroscopic, which means that it pulls water to the surface so that it quickly evaporates due to the heat emitted from the light bulb. This is one of the reasons salt lamps leak water in humid climates. When there is water vapor in the air, it carries bacteria, mold and allergens. Salt lamps draw the water vapor as well as the elements it is carrying to the surface of the lamp thereby removing it from the air. This is one of the most beneficial functions of a salt lamp.

A LOW-LAMP LIGHT MAKES A GREAT NIGHT LIGHT

According to research, the body is affected by different colors of light. It is recommended that blue light be avoided after the sun goes down because it can have a negative effect on the circadian rhythm, which disrupts sleep hormones.

The majority of light sources such as tablets, laptops, computers, TVs, and cell phones emit blue light and the majority of us spend hours on end staring at these screens, especially during the evening.

Salt lamps provide a warm orange light similar to the light that radiates from candlelight or a campfire. This is why they are a beneficial light source and can stay on throughout the night without interrupting sleep.

For those who suffer from seasonal affective disorder (SAD), soft orange hues increase focus, boost energy levels and calm moods. The negative ions also contain mood-enhancing elements.

CHAPTER 6: HOW TO PROTECT YOURSELF FROM ENERGY VAMPIRES

An energy vampire is a person who drains your energy; they are also referred to as energy suckers and psychic vampires. Some energy vampires are conscious of what they are doing and others are not. The unconscious are typically mentally ill or emotionally unstable; they have a desperate need to draw life from those who have healthy and strong energy. Empaths will usually feel dizzy or drained when energy is being drawn from them by a vampire.

There are also conscious energy vampires who have been trained by negative and dark forces to collect positive energy. They do this for several reasons: to gain recognition, power, boost their self-esteem, boost their ego and for youth or health.

It is essential that you protect yourself from energy drainers; here are some strategies to help you:

Don't Give too Much

It is good to give, as it enhances your psychic awareness, spiritual growth and your personal evolution. However, it is important that you replenish yourself every time you give; you need to master the balance of giving and receiving. When someone gives you something small, like paying you a compliment, receive it with an open heart and say thank you; there is no need to give back to them and respond with another compliment.

Refrain From People Pleasing

There are some people who will attempt to please everyone. This is simply not possible; we all have different frequency vibrations. You will attract those who you are on a similar vibration with and the others you will deflect. You can be your own energy vampire when you attempt to please everyone.

BE CAUTIOUS OF EGOTISTICAL PEOPLE

People who are only focused on themselves will drain you. When you have a conversation with them, all they can talk about is what they are doing and will ask how you are just as you are about to part ways. You will feel drained at the end of a conversation with them; limit your contact with or completely remove such people from your life.

BE CAUTIOUS OF NEEDY PEOPLE

Needy people do any and everything to get your attention. They are constantly asking for your help and advice but never apply it. These people will waste your time and drain your energy. Train yourself to know when you are dealing with such people and reduce the amount of contact that you have with them.

BE CAREFUL OF DRAMA QUEENS

These people are not difficult to detect because they are always involved in some type of problem. Everything that could go wrong does, and they are constantly bombarding you with emails, phone calls and text messages about the latest catastrophe in their life. Before you realize it, you will have no energy left. It is essential that you don't waste your time engaging with such people because they will destroy your field of energy.

Clarity

Don't waste time beating around the bush with people, get straight to the point. When a person is being too negative, shut them down; when a person keeps operating in the same behaviors and then asking for your advice, shut them down. If someone asks you to do something for them and you can't do it, just say so. You don't need to be rude, just be firm and let people know what your boundaries are so that they don't cross them.

Herb Smudging

Smudging involves the process of burning herbs to create a bath of cleansing smoke for the purpose of protection, purification and healing. Palo Santo Wood, also referred to as Holy Wood, is a type of sacred wood used by the indigenous people of the Andes and the shamans in Peru for purifying, medicinal purposes and to remove evil spirits. You can use cedar, sage and pine for smudging.

Gemstones and Crystals or Gem Elixirs

Quartz crystals, tiger eye, amethyst, tourmaline, obsidian and onyx are all used to protect against emotional distress, danger, psychic attack, empathy and oversensitivity.

Orgone

Orgone has several functions, including creating a protective energy field that surrounds your environment and your aura and deflecting negative energy. They are also used as a shield to deflect harmful pollutions and electromagnetic frequencies.

You should place four orgone protectors in the four corners of your home to protect against harmful energy and to ground spiritual energies. The Orgone Amulet of Protection provides protection against psychic attacks, bad vibes, emotional pollution and evil eye.

Candles

Candles remove negative energy from your home. They are also excellent for manifesting purposes. Dark blue, red and white candles are good colors to use for self-protection.

Resins and Incense

Incense made from natural substances such as frankincense, myrrh, sage, sandalwood, and musk are used to cleanse the atmosphere of homes and environments.

Baths

Add ½ cup of sea salt to your bath; this will cleanse negative energy that has attached itself to you after being in the presence of certain people. Steep a teaspoon of clove or basil into a cup of boiling water, strain the herbs out and add it to your bath; these herbs are known for their cleansing and protecting properties.

Protection Prayers and Chants

Any chants or prayers will work as long as they come from the heart using intensity, passion and determination.

CHAPTER 7: EMPATHS AND WORK

As an empath, you will face particular challenges in the workplace. Everyone deserves a job that fits their abilities and personality, but you need to take extra care before accepting a position because a toxic work environment can make you emotionally, spiritually, and physically sick – fast. So, as an empath, how can you pick the right kind of job and thrive at work?

ALWAYS ASK FOR A WORKPLACE TOUR BEFORE ACCEPTING A ROLE

When you go for an interview, ask whether you can take a tour if someone hasn't already offered to show you around. Pay attention to the employees' facial expressions, their body language, and the way they talk to one another. You'll quickly surmise whether the organization is toxic. Unless you are in desperate need of money, follow your gut instinct and avoid workplaces that contain a significant amount of negative energy.

Pay close attention to the lighting, the noise levels, the amount of clutter, and the layout of the desks. Ask yourself whether you could be comfortable working in such an environment, from both a physical and emotional perspective. A high salary might be enticing, but your health and sanity must come first. Even if other people tell you that a job is too good an opportunity to pass up, trust your intuition.

You have the power to make a positive difference in the workplace, but you are under no obligation to sacrifice your mental and physical health if doing so is beyond your comfort zone. Never feel bad about choosing the right job for you.

USE YOUR GIFT AS A SELLING POINT

Empaths are not show-offs by nature, and the prospect of selling yourself in a job interview might be enough to make you feel queasy. But think of it this way – your empathic qualities are actually an increasingly valuable commodity in the workplace. We tend to associate the business world, and even the public sector, with a kind of cut-throat mentality where everyone is trying to outdo one another and compete for the best positions and the most money.

However, our society is increasingly aware that taking care of one another and our planet is the only way forward. We still have a long way to go in creating a more caring world but, in general, we are starting to understand the benefit of a healthy work-life balance and the merit of cooperative working practices rather than a dog-eat-dog mentality. If you feel up to the challenge, you can use your gift to help drive this change!

You know that there is far more to life – and work – than status or salary. Your gift makes you perfectly suited to roles that require listening, conflict resolution, and mentoring skills. Psychiatrist, author, and empath Dr. Judith Orloff maintains that empaths bring passion, excellent communication skills, and leadership ability to their professional roles. When an interviewer asks what you can bring to a job, don't hesitate to give examples of times you have demonstrated these gifts.

Working Alone Versus Working With Others

Although you have strong leadership potential, a role involving extensive contact with colleagues and customers on a day-to-day basis may prove too draining, especially if you are not yet confident in your ability to handle negative energy and toxic individuals. Be honest with yourself when applying for a position. If it entails working as part of a busy team with few opportunities to recharge during the day, think carefully before making an application.

Most empaths are well suited to working for themselves or taking on jobs within small organizations. Working in a large office or noisy environment may be too stimulating – and that's fine! We all have different needs and talents, so do not allow anyone to make you feel inferior for not being able to handle a "normal" workplace. As an empath, you may quickly become overwhelmed by the prospect of having to interact with coworkers, members of the management team, and customers.

On the other hand, working alone can result in social isolation if you take it to extremes. If you decide to run a small business from home, for example, be sure to schedule some time with family and friends at least a couple of times per week.

Not only do you need to nurture your relationships, but it is also helpful to gain an outsider's perspective on your work from time to time. Sometimes, you may get so caught up in a project that relatively minor problems seem to take on a life of their own. Talking to other people allows you to take a more realistic view and help you come up with new solutions.

If Your Environment Drains Your Energy, Ask For Reasonable Adjustments

You can't expect your boss to redecorate the office just to suit your preferences or to fire an energy vampire, but you can ask them politely whether they would mind making a few small adjustments. For example, if there is a harsh strip light directly over your desk, you could ask whether it would be possible to turn off the light and use softer, gentler lamps instead.

If you work in an environment in which people talk loudly, experiment with white noise or other sound recordings designed to trigger feelings of calm and emotional stability. Try sounds recorded in nature, as these are often soothing for empaths. You can find lots of free resources on YouTube or specialized noise-generating sites such as mynoise.net. If possible, listen to natural or white noise via noise-cancellation headphones for at least a portion of your workday.

There are also additions and adjustments you can make that do not require permission from your boss. For instance, you can place crystals on your desk as a means of countering negative energy and set aside a few minutes each day – even if you are incredibly busy – to ensure your desk is clear of unnecessary clutter. If you work with a computer, pick a calming scene or color as your desktop wallpaper. Frame a photo or uplifting picture and keep it on your desk. Look at it for a few seconds when you need a dose of positive energy.

If you enjoy your job but would prefer to spend less time around other people, consider asking your manager whether you can work from home a couple of days each week. This can give you some respite from other peoples' energy and enables you to take a break at any time. Working from home comes with the privilege of setting up an environment that suits you perfectly. For example, you could install a water feature on your desk or play natural background noise throughout the day without fear of eliciting annoying questions from your coworkers.

Watch Out For Energy Vampires

If you come across an energy vampire in your personal life, you usually have the option of cutting contact with them, or at least limiting how much time the two of you spend hanging out. Unfortunately, this isn't the case when you are forced to work alongside them.

This is where boundaries come into play. You need to politely but firmly assert yourself from the outset of your professional relationship. Don't be drawn into petty workplace gossip, and don't accept any invitations from toxic people to socialize outside of work. Draw on your best energy self-defense skills, and always put your wellbeing before professional obligations.

Empaths who choose to work in the helping professions, whether with other people or animals, need to remain aware of the effect of their work on their energy levels. For example, if you work as a psychologist or therapist, speaking to a client who is going through an especially sad or difficult time in their life can leave you exhausted, depleted, and even depressed. Be sure to allow a few minutes between clients or appointments in which to ground yourself, and schedule plenty of time to relax and nurture yourself outside of work.

Draw A Line Between Your Workplace and Home

If you work outside the home, it's a good idea to devise a routine that creates a clear dividing line between your professional and personal life. As an empath, you are susceptible to carrying the negative energy of others with you. You may catch yourself worrying not only about the problems you are facing at work, but also those of your colleagues, bosses, and customers. Unless you learn how to "switch off," you will soon become overwhelmed, anxious, and depressed.

When it's time to wrap up your work for the day, stay mindful of the transition between work and home. Create a ritual that automatically encourages you to switch your focus to personal interests and feelings rather than those of colleagues and clients. For example, you may wish to spend the final five minutes of your workday in meditation or tidying your desk whilst listening to a particular soundtrack or piece of music. If you have a friend or relative who always raises your energy levels, you could get into the habit of texting them just before leaving work or on the way home.

Focus On How Your Work Helps Others

It isn't always possible to change your job or work in the field of your choosing. If you are stuck in a job that isn't right for you and are in no position to make a change any time soon, try approaching your work with a new mindset.

As an empath, you have a talent for helping others. Not only do they benefit from your support, but you also get to soak up their positive energy too. It's truly a win-win situation! Try to find opportunities to lend a hand to someone else, and offer emotional support as long as it doesn't leave you feeling too drained.

For example, if one of your colleagues seems especially stressed, take the initiative and ask them if they'd like to talk to you for five minutes about anything that's bothering them. Sometimes, just offering a listening ear can turn someone's day around! Or perhaps you could offer a more practical form of help. For instance, you could offer to take everyone's mail to the mailroom on your coffee break. Acts of service and kindness allow you to find a sense of meaning in your work, even if you are hoping to change careers in the near future.

Chapter 8: Normalizing and Maintaining Your Gift

Now that you have learned how to embrace and leverage your gift, the next step is to normalize it. This involves learning how to make the gift a normal part of everyday life. At this stage, you will no longer need to think about how you plan on responding or how you intend to use your gift, you will just be able to use it and reap the benefits from it. There will be no need to put any effort into the thinking about tapping into your gift; it will become like the air that you breathe.

The normalizing process is a crucial part of fully stepping into your gift as an empath. It will free you from worrying about the fact that you are an empath because now you are capable of managing it consistently. Never again will you have to worry that your gift has some type of hold over you because you now know what you need to do when things get out of control. You will be able to tune in and out of energy when you want to.

You will never become void of all the emotions that you used to feel; when you are normalized, you will only feel the emotions and energy that you want to feel. You will no longer pick up energy from other people or feel an immediate negative reaction to the energies that you are exposed to. Once upon a time, you might have lost your temper or become exhausted and drained because of negative energy. You may have avoided crowds, public places, certain people, dinner parties, family gatherings and house warming parties because you knew that you would leave feeling drained, overwhelmed and exhausted, which could last for several days. During that time, you were perplexed as to where these feelings were coming from, leading you to feel frustrated and irritated as a result.

Now that you have become accustomed to life as an empath, you no longer experience these negative feelings. You can walk into a room full of unfamiliar or familiar people and feel energized and empowered. You no longer absorb the emotions and energies from other people; you are still capable of reading their emotions but they no longer have the power to hold you hostage. You know how to ground yourself and deflect the feelings, energy and emotions that are not beneficial to you.

Maintain Your Gift

Maintaining and mastering your gift are two completely different processes. When you have mastered your gift, you find it easy to live in harmony with it and as discussed above, you have normalized it. However, don't get comfortable once you have reached the normalization stage because now you need to maintain your gift to ensure that you don't regress to the beginning stages of learning that you were an empath. There are several things that you will need to do to maintain your gift. This process will enable you to live in perfect harmony with your gift.

Regular Check In

To maintain your gift, it is important that you check in on a regular basis. You should do this a minimum of once a day, but you should really aim for twice a day. The best times to do so are first thing in the morning and before you go to bed. This will enable you to reflect on the things that have had the most effect on you throughout the day. In the morning, you are capable of recognizing residual experiences that you have been unconsciously holding onto. Much of what attaches itself to our minds often comes to life in our dreams; you can then let these feelings go and get on with your day in peace and harmony.

It is a good time to check in before going to bed because the experiences that you have had throughout the day will be fresh in your mind. You will be able to detect how these experiences have affected you and release them so that you can have a peaceful and restful sleep.

Daily Meditation

The best time to meditate is as soon as you wake up in the morning and just before you are going to bed at night. However, make sure that you don't make a habit of meditating until you fall asleep because this can have a negative effect on your meditation practices. It can leave an imprint on your unconscious mind causing you to associate meditation with sleeping, which will lead you to fall asleep during your meditation times in the morning and throughout the day. Meditating gives you the opportunity to rest with your energy. You don't have to feel as if you are in control; there is no stress and you can enjoy your energy at that moment.

Deep Breathing

It is important that you relax often, but at the same time, you should make sure that your breathing follows a certain pattern. Deep breathing allows you to relax completely by achieving a state of rest within your body. A good breathing exercise that you can try is to breath in for 4 seconds, hold your breath for 6 seconds and then breathe out for 8 seconds. This will help you eliminate any excess air from your body. At the same time as taking deep breaths, you can imagine any negative energy or stress leaving your body with the air.

Deep breathing is an excellent way of centering yourself and quickly gaining harmony within. If you ever find yourself struggling with your grounding exercise, begin to intentionally center your breathing. This will help you gain complete control over emotions and come back to your power center. It is advised that you practice breathing deeply daily and anytime that you find yourself in a distressing situation.

Intentional Grounding

An important part of normalizing your abilities as an empath is that you ground and shield yourself on a regular basis. The process of grounding allows you to regularly eliminate unwanted energy and intentionally come back to your center.

You should never leave maintaining your energy on autopilot because you will fall out of alignment very quickly and become unbalanced. Even when you have managed to master your abilities as an empath, you will still find that you get into situations where you are absorbing energy from other people.

CHAPTER 9: HOW TO SUPPORT A YOUNG EMPATH

You now know how to take care of yourself as an empath, and how to best use your gift. However, if you have a young empath in your life, it's important that you also understand how to support them. Children with this ability often face significant challenges, but your support can make all the difference as they come to terms with the fact that they are different from their peers.

Being an empathic child is tough, but young empaths have so much to offer our world, and they should be appreciated! Psychologist and empathy expert Dr. Michele Borba believes teenagers today are running low on empathy. In fact, they are only half as empathic as those of previous generations.

It's clear that young empaths have a lot to teach their peers.

How To Spot A Young Empath

Empathic gifts are present from birth, and young empaths have the same abilities and needs as empathic adults. However, because children have less experience in understanding and expressing their own emotions, their empathic nature may manifest in a different way.

Empathic children usually prefer to play alone or in the company of just one or two good friends. In general, they gain more enjoyment from talking and playing with older children and adults than those their own age. It isn't that they believe themselves to be superior to their classmates. Rather, a young empath's unusual maturity means that they are on the same wavelength as those older than themselves. They may report feeling distant or alienated from people their own age.

An empathic child may surprise you with their uncanny ability to hone in on what others are thinking and feeling. For example, you may be feeling stressed about an incident at work while cooking dinner for the family one evening. Your empath child might walk past the kitchen door and immediately discern that you are upset about something that has happened during the day. They may well give you a hug and ask you to tell them exactly what or who has made you sad.

It is important that you strike a balance between honoring their gift and overloading them with inappropriate information. If you are upset or angry, denying it will teach your child that their intuition cannot be trusted, which will instill self-doubt and confusion.

On the other hand, there is no need to share too many details, as this could cause them unnecessary distress. For example, a young child does not need to know absolutely everything about a serious illness or assault. A simple acknowledgment of the situation and the feelings that go with it will be sufficient in most cases. Do not lie to your child and keep discussions age-appropriate.

Uncover The Real Reasons Behind Temper Tantrums

Think carefully before chastising a young empath for bad behavior. Yes, they might be disobeying you simply because they are a naughty child, but they could also be acting out in response to overwhelming stimuli in their environment.

Consider the situation from a toddler's perspective. As an empathic adult, you can usually make your excuses and leave if you find yourself bombarded by too much noise or light. Unfortunately, a young child has less autonomy and often has no choice but to endure it. In a bid to protect themselves, they may either freeze up – which is why empathic children are often labeled "shy" – or they can attempt to regain control over the situation by causing their own noise and disturbance!

If you suspect that your child is an empath, do not be surprised if they suddenly act out from time to time. If they are having meltdowns or tantrums on a regular basis, it's time to dig a little deeper. Think like a detective. Are there any triggers that reliably predict "bad" behavior? Take your child's complaints seriously – if they tell you that they don't like strong light or smells, believe them!

Let anyone else who cares for your child know that they are an empath or, if this concept is alien to the person in question, that your child is unusually sensitive and requires a few minor adjustments. For example, if they attend a daycare center, you should let the staff know that they are liable to become overwhelmed during high-energy games and might require some time out to calm themselves down.

Under no circumstances should you shout at a young empath, use harsh punishments, or resort to abusive tactics such as name-calling. These approaches are destructive anyway, but when the child in question is an empath they are likely to cause long-lasting damage. If you lose your temper, apologize immediately. Take full responsibility for your own conduct.

CREATE SOOTHING ENVIRONMENTS

Make sure that an empathic child has a safe space they can call their own, and allow them to retreat when they need some alone time in which to relax and recharge their batteries. If they need to spend ten or twenty minutes in their room then let them, even if you have family or friends over.

Empathic children may require more time to wind down and get ready for sleep at the end of a busy day. Their nervous systems are more easily stimulated than those of typical children, and just telling them to get into bed and close their eyes is unlikely to result in a good night's rest!

It's a good idea to schedule a bedtime routine to help them relax. For example, you could prepare them a bath with calming essential oils, tell them a familiar bedtime story, and encourage them to reflect on the best things that happened that day.

HELP THEM PREPARE FOR THE HARSHER REALITIES OF LIFE

Caring for an empathic child can be heartbreaking at times because their gentle, kind hearts are easily bruised when they realize how much suffering exists in the world. They are also more susceptible to hurt feelings if and when an argument breaks out in their social circle. An empathic child might struggle to understand why other children seem to hurt one another because they could never behave in such a cruel manner.

It's natural and normal, as a parent or caregiver, to try to shield a child from pain. Unfortunately, although it may work in the short term, you will be doing them a disservice in the long run. An empath who is not taught how to work with their gift and handle their emotions early in life is at risk for depression, anxiety, and confusion later on when they come up against the harsh realities of the world.

You cannot solve the world's problems, but you can keep the lines of communication open with your child. When they pick up on signs of tension and emotional turmoil, whether it's at home or school, give them the chance to talk about it. Encourage them to express themselves fully – feelings are there to be felt, after all. It's far healthier to teach them coping strategies early on. This empowers them because they know that they can handle almost anything life throws their way.

GIVE THEM PRACTICAL TECHNIQUES THEY CAN USE

So how can you equip a young empath with the tools they need to thrive in a harsh world?

First, teach them how to meditate, and the importance of taking at least a few minutes each day to ground themselves. Children are more receptive to new ideas than adults, and you probably won't have to spend much time and energy persuading them to try it out. Why not schedule joint meditation time each day? This will not only help them develop a positive habit that will last a lifetime, but it will also deepen your bond.

Second, help them learn to verbalize their emotions, to give them a name, and understand how others' feelings exert a direct effect on their moods. Emphasize that it's important to choose healthy friends who are usually happy and to spend time with people who leave them feeling energized instead of down.

Unfortunately, empaths of all ages are favorite targets for energy vampires and abusers of all kinds. Teach your young empath how to build boundaries, to set their own standards for relationships, and to walk away from people who wish them harm. Make a point of telling them that they can always come to you if they want or need advice on how to handle a toxic friend or bully. Practice saying "No," and use role play to rehearse how your child can extricate themselves from difficult situations.

Model the kind of behavior you want to see in your child. Do not deny your own feelings, make time for yourself when you get overwhelmed, and draw firm boundaries when others try to take advantage of you. Children are keen observers, and they look to their parents and caregivers for guidance.

If you are living in a home where two or more people frequently get into fights, take steps to address the problem. Young empaths pick up on tension in their living environment, and this can result in serious psychological and physical illness. Family counseling may be necessary in some situations.

Teenage Empaths

The teen years are challenging for almost everyone, and they pose special challenges for empaths. It is natural and normal for teens to seek acceptance from their peers, to break away from their families, and create their own identities. It is normal to experience heightened, turbulent emotions during this period. However, normal teenage problems can spiral into long-lasting psychological turmoil for an unsupported young empath.

Peer pressure is a real problem for teenagers. In their desire to gain their peers' approval, they may agree to take part in risky activities such as drinking, smoking, underage sex, and reckless driving. Fear of peer rejection can drive even mature empaths to put themselves in danger. For their own protection, they must understand the importance of strong boundaries and saying "No." If they haven't developed this ability by the time they enter adolescence, don't worry. It's never too late to learn.

Depression, anxiety, and other mental health problems often surface for the first time in adolescence. This means that young empaths may have to deal not only with their own mental health problems but also those of their friends. As naturally caring individuals, they will feel inclined to offer a listening ear or shoulder to cry on. This is an admirable response, but the young empath can soon feel overwhelmed by the sheer strength of a friend's emotions.

A transparent, nonjudgmental approach is best. Educate your teen about the difference between normal teenage emotions and adolescent mental health problems. Teach them how to spot signs of mental illness in themselves and others, and tell them where and how to get help. Bear in mind that they might not feel comfortable talking to you, so tell them that you will not be offended if they choose to seek guidance elsewhere.

If they are supporting a friend, praise their kindness but, at the same time, emphasize the importance of setting personal boundaries. If their friend is draining their own emotional reservoirs, it's time to point them in the direction of professional help. Reassure your teen that they cannot be expected to "save" their friend and, sometimes, calling on the services of a qualified adult is the best step to take.

In summary, the early years of an empath's life are key to their wellbeing as adults. Young empaths quickly realize that they hold special abilities. If they are not supported by the adults around them, an empath can feel lonely or even alienated from others. Fortunately, with gentle guidance and nurturing, they will come to appreciate and enjoy their amazing gift.

Conclusion

There is much more to being an empath than what you have read in this book. This is only the tip of the iceberg. Your journey has just begun, and you will continue to grow in your gift, meet others, and read more to enhance your knowledge. When you are unable to control your gift, it can often feel like a curse; after all, who wants to feel continuously drained, unwell, and exhausted? It can be difficult for you to manage at first, but as you learn to embrace and have power over your gift, you will eventually learn how to use it to leverage and enhance your life. You may even decide to use your gift to better the lives of others. Many empaths use their gifts as a career and others prefer to be more secretive about it. Whatever you choose to do is up to you, and there is no right or wrong way to use your gift. The most important thing is that you understand that you are not crazy, there is nothing wrong with you and that you can live a happy and healthy life.

It is important that you don't get offended by people who don't understand your gift because it really isn't their fault. Unless the person is an empath, they will find it difficult to comprehend. People will judge you and accuse you of being over-emotional and sensitive, which isn't wrong, but when it is said in a demeaning way, it can be hurtful. It is essential that you learn to protect yourself against the unwanted energy from these comments.

I hope that you now have a better understanding of your gift and that you embrace every part of it so that your life is enriched day by day.

I wish you all the best on your journey!

Essential Oil Recipes for Anxiety

Quick and Easy Lavender Neck Rub

Ingredients

- 3 drops of pure lavender
- 1 teaspoon of fractioned almond or coconut oil

Directions

1. Combine the lavender oil, almond and coconut oil in the palm of your hands and rub directly onto your neck. You can also rub the mixture onto the soles of your feet; this is particularly effective before bedtime.

Men's Cologne

Ingredients

- 5 drops of cedarwood essential oil
- 3 drops of bergamot essential oil
- 2 drops of sandalwood essential oil
- 8 ounces of 70 percent alcohol

- Glass cologne tube or glass roll on tube

Directions

1. Combine all the ingredients in the cologne tube or glass roll, shake together thoroughly and use whenever required.

FRANKINCENSE AND MYRRH LOTION

This homemade body lotion made from a mixture of frankincense and myrrh is a fantastic recipe. Not only does it alleviate anxiety symptoms but it also hydrates the skin with essential nutrients and vitamins.

Ingredients

- ¼ cup of olive oil
- ¼ cup of coconut oil
- ¼ cup of beeswax
- ¼ cup of shea butter
- 2 tablespoons of vitamin E
- 20 drops of frankincense essential oil
- 20 drops of myrrh essential oil
- Plastic lotion dispenser bottles

Directions

1. Combine shea butter, beeswax, coconut oil and olive oil in a bowl.

2. Add some water to a large saucepan and heat over a medium temperature until the water starts to boil. Place the bowl into the saucepan and heat the ingredients at the same time as stirring the mixture.

3. Remove the bowl from the stove and place it in the fridge for an hour until it becomes solid.

4. Remove the mixture from the fridge and use an electric hand mixer to whisk the ingredients until fluffy. Combine the vitamin E and the essential oils and continue to mix.

5. Add to the plastic lotion dispenser bottles and store in a cool place.

LAVENDER SOAP HOMEMADE BAR

This homemade bar of lavender soap not only provides relief from anxiety but is also extremely beneficial for the skin. It's simple to make, free from chemicals and easy on the pocket.

Ingredients

- 20-30 drops of lavender essential oil

- Soap base
- 3 drops of vitamin E
- Decorative soap mold or oval bar molds

Directions

1. Add water to a large pan and heat it over a medium temperature until it starts to boil.
2. Add the soap base to a glass bowl and then place the bowl in the saucepan until the base has melted.
3. Take the bowl out of the saucepan and allow it to cool down. Add the vitamin E and the lavender and stir together thoroughly.
4. Transfer the mixture into a soap mold and allow it to cool down and become completely solid before removing it from the soap mold. Store the soap at room temperature.

CPSIA information can be obtained
at www.ICGtesting.com
Printed in the USA
BVHW030557281221
624937BV00005B/171